"Ethan McGuire's debut collection, 'split between tradition and progression,' showcases a young poet exploring forms and tones, histories and traditions as he seeks to traverse, in language, 'one thousand li of dreams.' His poems are at once religiously grounded and formally restless—as he himself explains, 'I throw myself into structure, / The structured darkness of the Tao.' Yet his impressive engagement with Eastern language and literature is quickened by a cultural command of Bob Dylan and Bluegrass, Lynyrd Skynyrd and Leonard Cohen. *Apocalypse Dance* will introduce readers to a new poet with great potential, his poems 'new things . . . connecting worlds.'"

—**AMIT MAJMUDAR**, author of *Three Metamorphoses*

"Ethan McGuire's *Apocalypse Dance* is built on poems of passion and devotion that draw on inspirations ranging from classical Chinese poetry and Gerard Manley Hopkins to Bob Dylan and Joni Mitchell. McGuire is also mindful of the music of his words in ways that place him among our best formal poets."

—**A.M. JUSTER**, author of *Wonder and Wrath*

Apocalypse Dance

Apocalypse Dance

Ethan McGuire

RESOURCE *Publications* • Eugene, Oregon

APOCALYPSE DANCE

Copyright © 2025 Ethan McGuire. All rights reserved. Except for brief quotations in critical publications or reviews, no part of this book may be reproduced in any manner without prior written permission from the publisher. Write: Permissions, Wipf and Stock Publishers, 199 W. 8th Ave., Suite 3, Eugene, OR 97401.

Resource Publications
An Imprint of Wipf and Stock Publishers
199 W. 8th Ave., Suite 3
Eugene, OR 97401

www.wipfandstock.com

PAPERBACK ISBN: 979-8-3852-4198-9
HARDCOVER ISBN: 979-8-3852-4199-6
EBOOK ISBN: 979-8-3852-4200-9
VERSION NUMBER 03/13/25

The epigraph from Dana Gioia's "Poetry as Enchantment" introducing Apocalypse Dance's *poems is used with permission from Wiseblood Books.*

The image on the cover is one of a series of woodcuts on laid paper by Christoph Murer, all bearing the title The Four Horsemen of the Apocalypse, *from his* Sacra Biblia *series, published 1630.*

For my father, my Virgil

"When men disregard the standard against which all things are judged, The Tao, by violating the fundamental truths of nature and the natural order, the sky turns dark and the light fades, the earth cracks and quits yielding fruit, the spiritual equilibrium is agitated, the rivers become bone-dry, and kings and princes grow feeble too soon, their kingdoms decaying."

—Lao Tzu, *The Tao Te Ching*,
translated by Ethan McGuire

"Poetic language expresses itself as a totality, not as a transparent vessel for conceptual content—just as music and dance express meaning in ways that are physical and sensory rather than analytical... When poetry loses its ability to enchant, it shrinks into what is just an elaborate form of argumentation."

—Dana Gioia, "Poetry as Enchantment"

Contents

Acknowledgements | ix
Biography | xiii

Part One
  A Prelude | 3
  The Warm Front | 4
  Disciple Dash | 5
  Lovers | 6
  Circles Interrupted #1 | 7
  Rushed Gods | 8
  Dry Bone Mountain | 9
  Yeah | 10
  The Expat | 11
  Nostalgia by Night | 12
  Dependence Ambivalence | 13
  F r a g m e n t s | 14
  Apocalypse Dance | 15
  A Sinner's Prayer: A Portrait | 16
  The Arrogants | 17
  Fantasma | 18
  Salt | 20

Part Two
  Home | 25
  Good Weather Bad | 26
  Thorn & Shout | 27
  Lemonade | 28
  Eyes | 29

Absence of Desire | 30
Damned Winter | 31
Burn Hollywood Burn | 32
The Way | 33
The Yellow Crane Tower | 34
Sundown Chapel | 36
The Old Gods | 37
Generational Malaise | 38
The Ripper | 40
Between the Hillocks | 41
Patient History | 42
Refugee Song | 43
Gratitude | 44
Sorrow and Words | 46
Hurricane Sally Aftermath | 48
Fever of the Tao | 50
My Generation | 52
Welcome to Eternity | 54

Part Three
A Coming Storm | 59
Mo(u)rning | 60
New Year's Eve | 61
Autumn Wind/Winter Rush | 62
Lover, | 63
Red Christmas Kettles | 64
December Sunset | 65
Conquest | 66
A Warning for the General | 67
PTSD | 68
Just Before Dawn | 69
The Earth Lives On | 70
The King & Queen of Neon | 72
Domnhall Drummer | 74
Welcome Back | 76
Circles Interrupted #2 | 78
The Bluegrass Players | 80

Acknowledgements

For help with aspects of *Apocalypse Dance*'s creation and construction and for advice on individual poems, the author would like to thank Krista Adams, Laura Allnutt, Elijah Blumov, Juliet DeMarko, David Hughen, Eric McDonough, Matthew Buckley Smith, Bre Stephens, Debra Stogner, Matt Wall, James Matthew Wilson, Chris Yokel, Jen Rose Yokel, and, most importantly, his mother, Peggy McGuire, and wife, Autumn McGuire.

The author also thanks the Capital Circle Courtyard Marriott employees in Tallahassee, Florida who saved an early *Apocalypse Dance* manuscript—filled with all kinds of uncopied notes and revisions—from the trash when he foolishly forgot it in his hotel room; they said the book looked intriguing, and they wanted to read it, but they happily returned it when he came back around inquiring hopefully.

The author of *Apocalypse Dance* is grateful to the editors of the following publications for previously accepting and publishing this collection's poems, sometimes in earlier versions:

Agape Review: "Welcome Back"

Anti-Heroin Chic: "The Bluegrass Players"

Before I Turn into Gold: "Disciple Dash" and "Salt"

Better than Starbucks: "Absence of Desire"

Black History & More: "Good Weather Bad," "Home," "Valentine Winter," and "The Warm Front"

The Blood Rag: "The Old Gods"

Bloodshed Review: "Dependence Ambivalence" and "Fantasma"

The Crank: "A Sinner's Prayer: A Portrait"

The Creativity Webzine: "Apocalypse Dance," "Damned Winter," and "Patient History"

Emerald Coast Review: "Hurricane Sally Aftermath"

Fevers of the Mind: "Absence of Desire," "December Sunset," "Disciple Dash," "F r a g m e n t s," "Good Weather Bad," "Home," "The King & Queen of Neon," "Mo(u)rning," "Red Christmas Kettles," "Salt," "Thorn & Shout," and "The Warm Front"

Flashes of Brilliance: "My Generation"

Hard Rain Poetry: "Sundown Chapel"

Inspire: "F r a g m e n t s"

The Legend: "The Earth Lives On" and "Refugee Song"

Life in the Time of Corona: "The Earth Lives On" and "Eyes"

Literary Matters: "Between the Hillocks"

Lothlorien: "Circles Interrupted #2," "A Coming Storm," "Dependence Ambivalence," "A Prelude," and "PTSD"

MW: "Between the Hillocks" and "A Warning for the General"

New Verse Review: translated excerpt from *The Tao Te Ching*, "Sorrow and Words," and "A Warning for the General"

Overcome: "The King & Queen of Neon"

Poems for Persons of Interest: "The Old Gods"

The Poetry Cove: "Gratitude"

The Poetry Pub: "The Arrogants" and "Salt"

The *Sleerickets* Podcast: "Sorrow and Words"

Vita Brevis: "Sundown Chapel"

Voegelin View: "Conquest," "Just Before Dawn," "Nostalgia by Night," and "Rushed Gods"

The author also previously published some of this collection's poems:

At his site *The Flummoxed*: "Apocalypse Dance," "The Arrogants," "Burn Hollywood Burn," "F r a g m e n t s," "Lemonade," "Lover,," "Red Christmas Kettles," and "Welcome to Eternity"

In his chapbook of art and poetry, *Songs for Christmas*: "Autumn Wind/Winter Rush," "December Sunset," "New Year's Eve," and "Red Christmas Kettles"

And in his poetry chapbook *Before Apokalypto*: "Circles Interrupted #1," "A Sinner's Prayer: A Portrait," "The Arrogants," the translated "The Bluegrass Players" epigraph from Basho, "Damned Winter," "December Sunset," "Domnhall Drummer," "Dry Bone Mountain," "The Expat," "Fantasma," "Fever of the Tao," "F r a g m e n t s," "Generational Malaise," "Lemonade," "Lover,," "Lovers," "My Generation," "The Old Gods," "The Ripper," "Sundown Chapel," "Thorn & Shout," "The Way," "Yeah," and "The Yellow Crane Tower"

Biography

Ethan McGuire is a writer and healthcare cybersecurity professional whose essays, fiction, poetry, reviews, song lyrics, and translations have appeared in *Blue Unicorn, The Dispatch, Emerald Coast Review, Literary Matters, The New Verse News, The University Bookman, Voegelin View*, and many other publications. Ethan is a contributing editor at *New Verse Review* and the author of two poetry chapbooks, *Before Apokalypto* and *Songs for Christmas: Twelve Poems and Pictures for Winter and Yuletide*. Ethan grew up in the Missouri Ozarks, lived in the Florida Panhandle on the Gulf of Mexico for twelve years, and is currently settled in Fort Wayne, Indiana with his wife and their children. To find Ethan, visit his website TheFlummoxed.com to contact him, see publication updates, read new work, and more.

PART ONE

A Prelude

Deep in the night
When falls a dark shroud,
Sins often happen
No man knows about.
Yet, somehow, God
Will always find out
What few men really
Ever want screamed aloud.

The Warm Front

A dirty, cloudy night turns into morning.
Morning reveals a sickly, sepia sky.

A cold front lumbered through this way a week ago.
A wicked sort of weather is approaching now.

Disciple Dash

After Leonard Cohen

I would run free with you
    if just on principle,

Although, as you know,
    running's not my style.

Your love has transformed
    me into a disciple,

Even if only
    for a little while.

Hello. So long! Good-bye.

Lovers

Adapted from the Greek of Plato

> τὴν ψυχὴν Ἀγάθωνα φιλῶν ἐπὶ χείλεσιν εἶχον
> ἦλθε γὰρ ἡ τλήμων ὡς διαβησομένη
> —As quoted by Diogenes Laertius in
> *Lives of the Eminent Philosophers*

Always my soul, sure, longs to merge
And mingle with the others' souls—
Within their breasts—
But only when I kiss them on the lips!

Just now, while kissing Agathon,
I felt my soul upon my tongue—
The troubled wench—
She wanted to pass over into him!

Circles Interrupted #1

Ice-cold springs bubble forth from the Earth,
And their overflow spills into creeks.
Creeks saunter on into rivers vast
Whose flowings fill rippling lakes of glass
And then turn into rivers again
Until they filter out through deltas,
Combining with various oceans.

Plains stretch far beyond the sight of men
And fold up into mountains reaching,
Mountains scraping superfluous skies.
Equalizing snowy peaks, canyons
Split the earth violently, deeply.
Fair valleys and hills rest in between.
Marring men's towers protrude between.

Rushed Gods

The shades of night engulf the beaming day
As metal, plastic cars race each free wáy.
    Was *our* life always fast?

The forlorn moon can't wait to have a word.
All nectar drains before the head is stirred.
The rising sun, which scouts for white egréts,
    Espies a funeral march.

Each track the DJ spins is short and loud.
Each night mourns for the pulsing, dying crowd.
If morning moves their bodies' broken dreams,
And they wake after spilling out their schemes,
    Will *their* gods even care?

Dry Bone Mountain

I feel the closest to my God
When I lie on the crests of hills,
Blessed by the sun's glorious beams,
My bones bared to His giving light.
Yet I still love the warmth of flesh,
So I throw my own flesh back on.

I shrug my muscles' heft around
My back and heave a mortal sigh.

I know God wants my struggling soul
Laid out, my dry bones naked, stripped,
But, flinching at the burning knife,
I wander these dear mountains, steep,
In halfway worshipping belief.

Yeah

Here I go, yeah, here we go around again:
    You're *there*, I'm here, and we are gonna sin.
Will it wait one day until the tables turn?
    You *know* I've got a face that's bound to burn.

I'll *get* what's mine, of this I'm very sure,
    'Cause *you* know just how this old body burns.

So let's raise a glass to our own love and war.
    Some *days* we feel our bodies might be more,
Yet I'll raise a glass up to the fires of Hell.
    I *could* avoid 'em, ah, but will I? Well. . .

The Expat

I tried to find the perfect place to live.
No place I went completely satisfied.
Every place I went had something to offend me.

Imperfect, I demanded perfection for myself.

Each land I knew, it had a dirty city.
Each home I found was too uncomfortable.
Each person that I met, I had to leave them cold.

Disloyal, I required loyalty to my own self.

Now deadly, fallen, I look back toward
    Each chance I squandered just to have a chance
        To set my roots in some good ground and do some good.

Passing meaning, my life held no meaning or purpose.

Nostalgia by Night

The night is young, but everyone is old
In this town's restaurants and whiskey bars.
I dream of fireside wisdom—truths retold—
Yet all I hear? Worn lies of girls and cars.

The night is young, but everyone is sore
In this pretending jazz club, Blue Guitars.
I'm looking for a pathway or a door;
They're absent in all of these au revoirs.

The night is young, and we're all unaware
Of any counsel in our repertoires.
Temptations—cheap—I can find anywhere. . .
But I feel more content now with this certain farce.

    Resigned to stalk the sidewalks of past lives,
    I turn downtown to date in haunted dives.

Dependence Ambivalence

After lines from Joni Mitchell, Sean Harris, and Brian Tatler

Oh, damn you, rogue, you red, red rogue,
I get so lonely when you're walking.

In France, I met a gorgeous vampire.
She taught my awkward feet to dance.

I learned my lessons so damned well;
She was a teacher good as hell,

But she left me alone inside a fire.
Her departure left me dead at heart,

. . . and so I retired. With swaying hips
She threw my body back into my shell.

So I will never venture forth again,
Will never dance and swing or sin again.

Am I evil?
        Yes, I am.
Am I evil?
        Am I a man?
                Yes, I am.

Fragments

After Bob Dylan and a line from Marcus Aurelius

Time is   A víolent ríver
with   An óverwhélming swáy,
and anything   Which énters thére
is brought   To síght and swépt awáy.

Now I lack   The dísposítion
to re-   Fléct on évery mistáke.
Like Adam, I   Endúre the síns
each of   My síns in túrn must máke.

Like wood chips from   A fállen trée
along   The Strúma pássing bý,
memories drift   Throughóut my bráin
like   A cánopy ónce held hígh.

I have sacrificed   The yóungest mén
and   The máidens tó my góds;
I have sunk   The sáving shíps
just   To lówer Strýmon's ódds.

So I can   Not héal the húrting
I   Have cáused by léaving for hére;
I cannot   Forgíve my own síns,
and   My sórrow is tóo uncléar.

Apocalypse Dance

If I am honest with myself I know
The world around me teeters on the edge
Of something great—for good perhaps. Or not.

    I only need to step outside my door
    To see my city and our sweat-and-blood
    Achievements. Some of which we earned, and some
    Of which we stole or halfway stole from gods
    Who lived within the boundaries of this land
    Before our mothers knew our fathers' names—
    These awesome, awful prizes which may vanish
    Before I even turn around again
    To value and appreciate their worth—

        Our city's hardest-won accomplishments.
        We may deserve to lose them now. Or soon.

We are, all of us here, together—dancing,
Ignoring our collective shivering moment,
In time with tunes that oscillate between
The chilling and the fiery—engaged in dance
With no one other than Apocalypse.

A Sinner's Prayer: A Portrait

God, I do not believe in who You are—
Not, "Help my unbelief," but, "I'm untrue."
Come heal me, give me grace. I'm not that far

Away from Heaven now—some foreign star. . .
Forget it, Lord; I love a man—not You.
God, I do not believe in who You are.

Some women, too, still fill my mind and car.
I feel a thrill with each new rendezvous.
Come heal me, give me grace. I'm not that far.

Wild, evil thoughts cut through my mind. The scar
You see here on my brain, it is not new.
God, I cannot believe in who You are.

My wife, for years, has been my registrar.
She lets me know our youngest has no clue,
So heal us, give us grace. We're not that far.

"Forgive me?" I ask in my wife's boudoir—
Not mine, but why? I can't tell even You.
God, I do not believe in who You are,
But heal me, give me grace. I'm not that far.

The Arrogants

I feast on the leaves as they grow in the forest.
Descending to earth, I shall swallow the flames.
I take what is mine—it's a debt if you owe it.
I never have faltered in feeling the agony.

Now I set my sights on the hill of the wise ones;
In towers of men, they're dividing our world,
And ever their *tall* minds are doubled inside.
I break down the doors, and I worry their mirth.

There is not a height I will not climb to throw
A name from a mountain to place mine instead.
True, honest lies matter to no one, the farce
Will outperform all as we fall on our crowns.

For I am the fire, and I am the rain.
I rose from the earth, and I'm falling anew.
I will only blame you if *you* don't know *my* star,
For this is my story, and I'm unashamed.

No matter what happens now, I'm unafraid.
Hell, nothing else matters, for *un*controlled I shall remain.
I'll walk through the fire; I'll run through the flames.
I am, and forever I feel, unashamed.

Fantasma

I saw you just now—
Among the trees to the right of my door
As I stepped outside to walk your Lab;
I saw you the same way I often have
(When fallow sleep sends tendrils of fog through my brain
And eyelids grow heavy, over my eyes);
For moments, I caught your outline in the grove
—And I wished you were dead.

I saw you just now—
As I pressed myself between crowds on the street,
Hurrying upstream like a salmon,
And the darkly-clothed people were a salmon run,
But I spotted you at the edge of my vision,
And you stood there, still, for a solemn second,
Yet when you turned, you were a stranger
—And I wished you were dead.

I saw you just now—
Standing like a Watcher at the foot of my bed;
I started and jumped, straight up, alarmed;
You faded to the corner, paused for a ghastly minute,
Hooded and formless, hovering between two worlds;
My skin crawled as if to leave its body for good;

Oh, how every hair stood at rapt attention
—And I wished you were dead.

Did I ever wish you were dead in life?
I dare not think it, if I ever did.

Salt

A rock pillar of salt awaits those looking backward—

As a staunch evangelical American,
Once I epitomized a top-rung Christian.

You have asked me to discuss the future,
Yet we cannot discuss what has not been.
Leonard saw the future, called it murder,
The same as our own present and our past.

My upward way is at once my downward.
The downward path, it rises up likewise.
God sees all time present for forever.
I am not God; the night still spreads outside.

I struggled long in lost worldview warfare.
My weary back I never once unbent.
Then one night, along the troubled pathway,
A stranger told me he could build those walls:

> The walls between my culture and comfort,
> Walls between the foreign and family.

I sold my soul, crossroads, to the Stranger,
Though, true, he did not ask explicitly,

Only asked for proof of my loyalty,
And my tired soul I volunteered in pledge.

My upward way is at once my downward.
The downward path, it rises up likewise.
God sees all time present for forever.
I am not God; the night still spreads outside.

Once you sell your soul, lightning seals the deal.
Even when the pendulum oscillates,
Your soul is sold. You cannot buy it back.
I offer passers futures and my life.

> As I lie in the mud of dirty roads,
> Even the Stranger mourns my fate in time.

I lie trampled underfoot, Stranger of Gold.
I gave myself to you, oh my paper stranger.

—*I turn into a pillar of salt looking backward.*

PART TWO

Home

Cross-legged
Alone, 24,901
Miles from home.

Good Weather Bad

Red sky at night,
    Sailors delight.

Great, gray billows
    Brush over good news.

Thorn & Shout

The Queen, my queen—
Queen of the South—
Inspires our love
And a triumph's shout.

The King, my king—
King of the North—
Sits on a throne
Of thistle and thorn.

Lemonade

It's life and people throwing lemons,
    and my friends say,
        "Make some lemonade!"
But I require sugar,
And I require water,
Yet in the middle of this desert
I ain't got even bread, nor store to pay.

Eyes

Two eyes peer at me
Over the top of a mask:
A blue, surgical mask in
Its first public appearance.

Are the lips smiling?
Are the lips stretched in a frown?
Or, worse than either, are those
Hidden lips ambivalent?

Absence of Desire

Incredibly tired.
Painfully far beyond strained.
Absence of desire.

Fields of intense drought
Amidst acres of plenty.
Absence of desire.

Stark, spiderweb limbs,
Leafless, sporting icicles.
Absence of desire.

Worn, run, overwrought;
Unplowed, never left fallow.
Lifeless until Spring.

Damned Winter

The Winter was   too warm.

The season was   too short.
The rain was rare- ly ice.
The blanket spread   too thin.

The seeds made sprouts   too soon.
Tree blossom flow- ers froze.
The earth was not   quite cold

Enough to rest   the World.

Burn Hollywood Burn

After a line from Public Enemy

In our Democratic Age
Of the Internet, a star
Is born every day.

In our Democratic Age
Of the Internet, a star
Dies off every day.

The gods must have seen our world
And, jealous of man-made stars,
Carved Silicon Valley.

Burn, Hollywood, burn?
Burn Hollywood? Burn.

The Way

The clarity unclear—
The mercy by condition—
The charity severe—
The punishment perdition—

The law seems inconclusive—
The judgement inconsistent—
My faith is still elusive—
The enforcement damned persistent—

The knowledge bringing pride—
The way is in the word—
The suffering inside—
The voice remains unheard—

The truth is comprehensive,
But I am apprehensive.

The Yellow Crane Tower

From the Chinese of Cui Hao

Long ago, the wise one rode
    the yellow crane, from here—

The Tower of the Yellow Crane
    is all he left behind.

When yellow cranes depart a mountain,
    they do not return,

Not for one thousand years, while endless
    clouds drift through the wind.

The flowing Yangtze River mirrors
    Hanyang trees—too clear.

The scent of Parrot Island grasses
    shakes my mind—

the sun

Is setting: which path leads, through dusk,
    to my old hometown gate?

The river brings a melancholy
   mood . . . its mists entwined.

Sundown Chapel

I stumbled into the sanctuary,
And held my head up, wary, wary.
"Now, I know everything I need to know!"
I couldn't see a priest or pastor.
"Ah, never have I sought a master. . .
But *these* pews may have something, still, I lack."

The setting sun through stained glass windows. . .
It almost made me think of widows—
The ones, in life, who wandered past my path.
"Have I done what is right and needed,
As I have for myself succeeded?
May *be* these pews have something, yet, I lack."

I stumbled out of the sanctuary,
My head held so low, weary, weary.

The Old Gods

After Matthew Buckley Smith

I

God sits upon His throne, that golden height,
And holds worlds in His palms, withholds His might.

The Muses by His side both come and go
And whisper in our ears the good we know.

II

Old Satan rules the bowels of Earth's black flame
And wields his damned, wild reign, the King of Shame.

The Furies scour the land and boil men's blood
With coals—and with knives loose a crimson flood.

The Fates dispense and cut threads they contrive
And make men meet mean ends or come alive.

III

The Wyrd King Death on tertiary throne
Will flay his planet till all flesh is bone.

Generational Malaise

We
Fall
Naked.
We are free,
I swear, God, we are.
We alone will choose our shackles.

Void
Words,
Our own,
Echo back.
Our shouts gain our praise.
We are free, I am sure as Hell.

We
Live.
We lust.
We exist
To find a balance
Between free love and abstinence.

Must
. . . We
Choose Christ

Or Buddha?
Choose Friedman or Marx?
Yet we are independent, God.

Life
Pays
Back dues.
Our parents'
Rebellion became
Unearned wealth. Now life has arrived.

Sins
Fade
Away
In New Worlds,
Yet sins revisit
Their creators, to haunt, to burn.

We are not lost in your Hell.
We simply wander in search,
Some kind of Heaven to find.

The Ripper

Give it up now. Run. You can't hide,
Can't hide the ache etched in your side.
The things you've done, they're really yours.
You say, "That man down a few doors
Caused all of this," but, no. You've died.

You're withering slowly inside
From the weight of the loves who have sighed.
You laugh as if that's "usual course,"
But I know what's cut from your soul.
Give it up now.

The bláck graves hold billions who lied
To *them*selves, their own hearts defied,
Then turning their eyes from the source
Of very soul-death, willing, forced
That soul and that justice to collide.
Yet there's still a chance to be whole.
Give it up now.

Between the Hillocks

From the Chinese of Yue Fei

> "A gentleman does not part with his qin without good reason."
> —THE BOOK OF RITES

Last night,
The air was ice, but crickets kept on chirping through the cold.
They woke me from one thousand li of dreams—
I saw the third watch moon.

Shivering, I stepped out to pace the silent courtyard, alone—
I could not see a soul.

The moon outside my curtains shone like silver—
"Silver is the mark of honor," I thought.

Experience, ancient hills, old pines, bamboo—
These block my journey home.

I wish I could express my worries on the guqin, dear. . .
But these days my friends are few,
So who would listen to my broken strings?

Patient History

After Amit Majmudar

The doctor—Swift, a specialist, I think—
He really only babbled on and on—
Not like a brook which chuckles over stones
But like old fingers on a keyboard's keys.

He spelled out his dire diagnosis, fast,
With complicated sentences and words,
Yet it translated, all, to me as this:
Only, "It is what it is," and, simply, "Well,
These sorts of things will happen sometimes," too.

I walked out of his office with a haze
Completely interlaced throughout my brain.
That irksome lump my wife had pointed out—
The aches, the weariness which woke me up—
If I had been the type to bother folks,
Perhaps we could have caught this sooner then.

Still, no, that never was my way at all,
So I guess I'll just drive home and tell my wife,
For I have always quietly endured
The good and bad news sent to me by God.

Refugee Song

I see the wind roll waves across the plain.
I see the jungle when it's slick with rain.
I see the wildfires scorch the hills again.
    I don't remember them at all.

I see dust devils dance the desert sand.
I see tornadoes twist a scattered land.
I see a hurricane, with fear, expand.
    I let them go when evenings fall.

I see the highways fill with screaming cars.
I see the cities stretch their wondrous scars.
I see the bright, rich goods of strange bazaars.
    Each is some sight I can't recall.

I see my children as they race our trail.
I see my mother search for food and fail.
I see my wife her deep desires curtail.
    I make my memories banal.

    I see my home before it fell to flame.
    I see my people whisper our cursed name.
    I see community I can't reclaim.
        We wander; I remember all.

Gratitude

For C.C. & M.BS.

All my words fall short.
The truth is I know nothing new or novel.
  Should I express my gratitude to life?
  Should I express a Nietzschean embrace
    Of suffering—for life?

   Sure, I could sing the great uplifting songs,
   But each of them must end,
     And yet the world and life and suffering. . .
   These never end.

    So I throw up my hands, toward the sky,
    And I can only scream.
    "God damn!" That's all I have
    To make me feel alive,
    To make me feel I am a man.
    To me, this feels extreme;
    Beyond me, it is little—and a lie.

   Speaking to my soul,
     Admonishing, "Don't grow too weary yet.
   Go on ahead and lift your songs to Heaven."

Perhaps there is a lion's lungs within
My chest: "So scream to Heaven!"

No—damn it all to Hell!—it isn't much,
But I have nothing else
Fit for a man, a woman, or myself—
No, nothing else.

Sorrow and Words

From the Chinese of Li Qingzhao

Note after note, a long song—
Singing Autumn sorrow—

Searching. Searching.
Seeking. Seeking.

Quiet. Quiet.
Chilly. Chilly.

Mourning. Mourning.
Crying. Crying.
Downcast. Downcast.

Today, the air was warm, but soon the cold returns.
I feel that I may never rest.

Three cups—or more—diluted wine are warm,
Yet wine is insufficient to resist
Persistent evening winds.

The wild geese pass through—
They batter my heart too,
Even though I knew them well in the old days.

The foxglove blossoms pile in heaps around the garden—
So thin, all withered, worn.
No one desires to pick them now and bring them home.

Alone, I keep watch at the window,
Biding my time until the night I crave comes creeping.

Fine rain breaks up my watch and glazes wutong leaves
Until the dark arrives. . .

Drip. . . Drip. . .
Drip. . . Drip. . .

Sorrow—
Can I describe this world of pain
And this old melancholic mood
In any truth with only one dull word?

Hurricane Sally Aftermath

Billboards with canvases ripped up and dangling—
Pine trees snapped at their centers like toothpicks—
Power lines straining under magnolias—
Traffic signs, jagged, torn centers like paper—
Men dotting rooftops and stretching blue tarps—
Semis in ditches, on their backs like turtles—
A three-mile bridge collapsed in the center—
       Driving down the interstate, bare,
On our way to the marina, after the hurricane.

A church with its steeple bent over and broken—
Street saplings bowing toward cars on the road—
Ancient oak canopies blocking park pathways—
Jon boats and pontoons, on streets, resting, inland—
American flags, halved, at their poles flapping—
New paint chips stripped from the sides of old houses—
Conquistadors, bronze, fallen in fountains—
       Navigating cars stalled downtown,
On our way to the marina, after the hurricane.

Barges washed up and dry, squatting by condos—
Piers' timber supports holding up nothing—
Wooden docks, wayward, strewn about, splintered—
Two white yachts resting on wedding lawn venues—

The mast of a sailboat impaling an office—
Black petrol water washed through a bank's lobby—
Odd tombstones of boat's bows lining lagoons—
    Traversing the mournful wreckage
Of an abandoned marina, after the hurricane.

Fever of the Tao

After lines from C.S. Lewis, Sylvia Plath, and James Alan

> "The rebellion of ideologies against the Tao is a rebellion of branches against the tree."
> —C.S. Lewis, *The Abolition of Man*

Twisting, turning through the ether,
The past, the present, the future
Collide inside the very midst
Of what has been, what is, will be.
Time and space merge within and merge among
The varied planes of width, depth, and length,
Even breaking through to strange planes other.
The universe stretches past knowledge,
And time as we do not know it will never end.
Never will I know another, never.

Twisting, turning through the ether,
Persisting considerations,
Disturbing questions, hang pending.
My mind sees and does not see gods.
I am alive; I am alive, survive.
I hunger and I criticize lies,
The shadows of night, paranoid limits.

Pursuing my truth, pursuing truths,
I live to die; oh, God, give me life beyond mine.
Never will I love another, never.

Twisting, turning through the ether,
I throw myself upon mercies.
I throw myself into structure,
The structured darkness of the Tao.
The moss of trees becomes the moss of trees.
I observe the same thing every day,
Yearning to find my world's, nature's, order,
Longing for paths, ways, roads, for doctrines:
The reality of life before description.
Never will I need another, never.

My Generation

I

This is me, my generation.
This is me, taking a stand.
Yet toward what goal, I ask,
Will I fight until the end?

II

Everything I know is real,
Does it depend on my perception?
What if I cannot own my mirror image?
What if I could not talk or breathe?
Some tell me, "You can't really know a thing,"
But I must ask them, "How can I then trust your voice?"

This is me, my generation.

New Babel's towers falling down,
Their statues turn to dust in sand,
The ancient pyramids rise to the clouds,
But "Why?" is all that comes to mind.
My lovers tell me, "Let your heart decide,"
But is it love or lust if *I* love to get high?

This is me, my generation.

The Buddha's figure in a mill,
Old minds dividing on Olympus,
Three crosses carved, I lose uncertain thought.
A stranger breathes, "Life after death. . ."
I need some one just to lend me two eyes.
My God, some one, help me, my day's a twilight eve.

III

I need some one to show me just one way,
Some one to lead me out of this black afternoon.
I need some one, if just to lend me sight.
Some one, please, help me, as my days drift to the ocean.

This is me; this is my generation.
This is me, and I know we must take a stand.
Yet toward what goal will we fight 'til the end?
This is us, so join our mass. . .
This is me, my generation.

Welcome to Eternity

Welcome to eternity,
This is just the first day of your life.

Welcome to eternity,
This is where we dream of fear and lust. . .

The fire burns, the flame concerns,
The soul is black inside your heart.

Your mind goes numb, your head grows ever young
As you're descending through the dark.

Welcome to eternity,
This is the last day of your life.

Now everything you've ever done
Comes back to haunt you in these ages.

The ghosts of ages past are here to craze you now
Like the philosophers told you they might.

The ghosts of lifetimes past are here to haunt you now
Just as your teachers said they would.

Welcome to eternity.
Down here no drug will ease your mind.

No pill or shot was ever made
Could take away what evil hides here.

Friend, you must let it go, what can you do?
You have lost all presumptuous control.

They'll burn you slow; they'll roast you so,
They'll never cease until your body's charred.

As the things you've done come out
To thrill you, haunt you, cut you, spill you
Just like the preacher said they would.

As the misremembered things you've done,
They eat you up and spit you out
And throw you on the fearsome coals.

Come to me, embrace me. I am your tormentor,
Your persecutor, martyrdom-enabler.

Pray to God across the chasm ahead.
Pray that God will send a cavalry of thunderclouds
To wash away this world of fire.

Purgatorium,
    Infernum,
        Aeternum.

This is eternity.
Welcome to eternity.
This is only the first day of your time here...

PART THREE

A Coming Storm

The gods are moving furniture around,
    Above the thumping, shuddering clouds,
    As we look on from below in fear
        And joy.

Mo(u)rning

Not long ago,
    Not often in my mind,
My purpose was left unaccomplished;
    Come now (I may),
        Search fields to find
What in my blind moments I missed.

New Year's Eve

Let the wind whip the world's bones,
Let the snow build into banks,
Let our earth freeze beneath ice,
Green spring will arrive in her time.

Autumn Wind/Winter Rush

What rush
Of cat's patter,
In groaning/sighing trees,
Wispingly dances the forest?
The wind.

What joy,
With death's beauty
In multi-colored paint,
Is splashed across shrugging treetops?
Autumn.

What hope
Can come leaving
All green behind for brown?
The soil—like all life—needs sweet rest:
Winter.

Lover,

After Bob Dylan

One more night. There is an end I have in sight,
Even though it may be black as it can be.
   Well, I hope to see you there;
   No, it will not matter what you wear,
And for tonight your light is all I need,
Because tonight our love is all I see.

Red Christmas Kettles

I turn my collar up against my town,
Thrust icy fingers deep into my jeans,
And shrug my jacket tighter 'round my frame.

I hunch my shoulders then resign myself
To plunge into the changing winter's fog
And stride the dirty streets, averting eyes.

I turn my troubled thoughts against my town,
Until Salvation Army Santas stand
To ring their bells and shiver through their smiles.

December Sunset

The sun is setting,
The cold is coming,
And yet the falling sun
Still shines with glórious rádiance.

A day is ending,
A night is nearing,
And yet the night, to me,
Is nothing to be feared.

My work is over,
My time must answer...
True, but I do not mourn,
Because the sun helps show:

To thé day-lover,
Let nó thoughts linger
On thé shadóws of night,
For thé sun rises áfterward.

Conquest

The oceans speak of power, might, design.
I sit upon this cliff-top now and mourn
At tales the oceans tell to my decline.

They tell me of the ships they love to scorn.
They laugh regarding sailors they have drowned.
They cough up all the pieces they have torn.

Then noticing a silence—much of sound!—
I hear no more the waves lash at cliff-shore,
And heavens—looking to the clouds—resound.

The tale, it loops around the green-spread moor,
And stretched-wide arms reach out to welcome me
As sages tell me of triumphant lore.

My hands have been destroyed by cruel sea,
But, looking back, a rising hand I see.

A Warning for the General

After the Chinese of an unknown Song Dynasty Chinese sage who is said to have warned General Yue Fei via an esoteric poem of his impending death

The waters underneath the storm pavilion surge,
And they will bring ten thousand hardships with their churn.

When you set out to sail those waters, hold the rudder firmly,
Be always wary of your traveling companions,
And push the body down until you are next to the Tao.

To reach the last day of the year is not enough.
When heaven cries, two points to poison people come.

The treacherous old man still moves around—why pester people?
His bumblings may soon be stopped, but soon enough?
Be careful now. Be sure to watch the sails and watch the storm!

PTSD

While dying on this field of glory,
I find no wounds have found my flesh.
Here, you and I alone are victors—
Our battle here crushed all who thresh.

Our souls are thrust through with the bludgeon
Of anguish, cries, and blood, and gore.
The two of us emerge from blood pools
Which drowned what good we knew before.

Our war, doomed, here we could not squander;
The ones we fought for clutched us tight,
And yet our tears mingle in mud;
We hold each other close tonight.

The people here can never know
What nightmares trouble nights, our day:
The screams, the smells of bright life leaving
That ever appear in our way.

Now, you and I, well, know each other.
We understand our troubled souls.
I ask you, stay and help me deter
The death that seeks to keep me low.

Just Before Dawn

Here in my darkest hour, I lie grasped
Among the roots of damp and mossy oaks
While overlooking black alfalfa fields,
Above which coming fogs will linger long
And float suspended there.

Before my sight, the mists rise from the grass—
Out of green, bowing blades and stems—and drift
Above too many weeds, scattered throughout.
This hollow, my own resting place, has been
So silent for the last few hours, calm
Before a new sun rise.

Rough nature, under autumn's outstretched wings,
Sits unconcerned with raging fire tongues
Out in an unseen distance just beyond
The far horizon, cedars-broken, dry.
I see the smoke . . . almost.

I crouch, observant—bark crags at my back,
Rough, rippling, as is throughout these woods;
They prod me and they, also, feel alive—
And begging God for clarity, I pray.
I pray my blood will slowly become calm,
Be neither ice nor fire.

The Earth Lives On

A star burns hot in the universe.
Ninety-three million miles away,
A lively planet slowly circles:
    The Earth, and the Earth lives on.

Men scar the Earth's complexion, building
Ziggurats, pyramids, Babel,
Steel skyscrapers, reaching fingers.
    The Earth sighs; man's work crumbles.

Men assemble machines for pleasures.
Men steer machines to kill others,
Shooting through the sky, exploding.
    The Earth breathes and brings a calm.

Men lift kind populists to power,
And populists aid their people,
But corruption's rot ever creeps.
    The Earth rules to heal the rot.

Authoritarians convince men,
Convince people of their power,
Erecting bold statues to boast.
    The Earth waits; the statues fall.

Populations grow, intermingle.
Viruses put fires to countries;
The fires spread fast through continents.
    The Earth brings rain to the flames.

Women birth men; men live, and men die.
Women give birth to men again.
Man is haughty, and he is so strong.
    The Earth, she spins forever.

The King & Queen of Neon

He leans on the wall;
She rests on the tacky bar—
Yellow lights flashing.
He's too old to haunt these clubs;
She ignores her date who whines.

He searches the crowd;
She peers through the throbbing throng—
Orange lasers piercing.
She catches His eyes and stares;
He longs toward Her but remains.

Across the alley—
Running with urine and beer—
Red-shaded bulbs light
A Thai place where two couples
Lean back at thin, dim tables.

He sits with a girl
Who only keeps texting friends,
Whose glasses shine white.
She sits across the room, slouched;
Her date fidgets with a watch.

Another night club,
This The Downtown Denizens—
Purple lights flashing.
He and She dance, moving, smiling,
Lips open without speaking.

She rolls with the song;
He circles Her and holds on—
Blue lasers piercing.
They laugh and their feet grow tired;
They tumble out together.

He drinks a jack 'n' coke;
She drinks a vodka cran.
Her green dress sparkles.
Hand in hand, they waltz with skill;
Hand in hand, they take a drink.

Domnhall Drummer

Domhnall Drummer had walked on the backs of men so long
His step had grown accustomed to their rolling.

  His government cared not if men did wrong,
  Cared not for rich men but did never mind
  If men got rich, if those men minded *them*.

  First Domhnall carefully just pushed and pranced
  Upon the backs of few to test their measure,
  But when sight told him, he mowed men on down,
  When sight said they held penchants for his rule.

  Old Domnhall lived too many vampire years,
  So brute-like, stealing blood and gaining life.
  All men who bowed and let him fall his feet
  Upon their shoulders had but none else to them.

  No *true* man loved old Drummer in his heart,
  Though some men liked the money that he gave them.
  No *true* man liked his ways, or his mean methods.
  Yet most men made old Drummer feel secure.

    "Mr. Drummer sees the future surely!"
    "Domhnall Drummer sure knows how to bargain!"

"Mr. Drummer seems a dangerous man!"
"Domhnall Drummer is no longer here!"

Domhnall Drummer had walked on the backs of men so long
When one stood up, Domhnall slipped and broke his neck.

Welcome Back

In response to Neil Young and Crazy Horse

The stars spread through the night,
They only know we see them there,
Pinpoints of light stuck through
A thick, black canvas stretched across
The Heavens, bold as day.
Intuiting we follow them,
Stars burn their hottest flame.

Orion is my friend.
I seek him at my loneliest,
Seek just to see his hunt
Throughout the forests, shimmering.
I follow his bright belt
And know brave Sirius's light
To run beside the Dog.

When troubles spill my soul,
The stars are my mute confidantes—
For words God understands
Yet I wish no man else to hear—
With pitiful wood fires
Of pine to kindle, oak to burn,
Lit near my prostrate frame.

Perhaps I am a fool
To walk in comfort with the stars.
The night holds terrors still
Which I fear little, because light
Lies thrown upon my path.
God, even so, my hollow heart
Fills only half the way.

Since stars know we see them
But they cannot see us—cannot
Reach down to fill our hearts—
They are our lips-sealed confidantes,
Because they have no tongues,
Remaining gods without much voice,
But my soul longs for more.

Circles Interrupted #2

After lines from Bill Monroe and Bob Dylan

The Devil appeared, one afternoon,
In my cabin home among the hills.
He flew me atop a mountain high.
Having never seen more than the hills,
Happily I followed quickly there,
Leaving my crying wife and babies.
"I'll be back soon," I whispered to them.

"Every single thing you see is yours,"
Satan said unto me then, "Only
We have a few battles to fight now.
Mother Earth suffers at human hands.
Only you can free her from their grip,
If you will but help me spill the blood
Of every man who charges these plains.

"The dirt will grow red with their bad blood,
And new flies will cloud their visages,
And one million men more may well come,
But natural armies will prevail.
If you shall, I offer you, lead them."
Thus the Devil tempted, seductive,
As I gazed in wonder at the Earth.

He appealed to the rage I have felt
Long at the oppression of humans,
Those who oppress my people and lands,
Locking us in their train's red caboose,
So cutting them down sounded perfect...

Yet with Satan here, God was somewhere,
And my babies' cries filled up my ears.

The Bluegrass Players

> While waiting out a storm at Ōishida, I found the scattering winds had blown the seeds of haikai there which had taken root in the villagers' minds. The resulting vines were bearing sweet perennial flowers. The smell brought back old times and softened the heart—like the clear notes of a flute. Yet the village poets were lost in the forest of error, unable to distinguish between the old and new ways, trying to take both at once without anyone to guide them. I sat and composed a collection of linked verse with them, leaving it as a gift, trying to be of some help during my own travels.
>
> —Matsuo Bashō, *The Narrow Road to the Deep North*, translated by Ethan McGuire

My father, driving down I-44—
Still peering through his wipers and the hárd rain—
Reached over to the dial, searching for
At least one halfway decent Country station.
He took his eyes off of the road to laugh
And say to me, "Ah, now, that is the stuff!"

The 107.9 Coyote at the Lake
Played mostly boring mainstream slop.
Today was different though—Southern Rock
For one whole hour: ZZ Top,

The Ozark Mountain Daredevils, or Lynyrd Skynyrd,
Molly Hatchet—Dad just stroked his beard.

I chuckled then and said, "It would appear
We're listening to good ole Rock 'n' Roll
On our way to play Bluegrass here!"
Dad furrowed his thick brows and said, "Well, on the whole,
This music has much more in common
With Bluegrass than this station usually can summon."

We played a Bluegrass show with Uncle Malcolm's band,
And afterward we jammed, as was expected,
But only joined as long as we could stand.
The guys who stayed were split, affected
By both the old and newer ways of playing,
Without a master's guiding hand—for staying.

My father and my uncle stood around
And talked as we packed up our instruments,
But even there, as thoughtful and profound
As they still are, their interlocutors
Fell damned far short (of those two intellects):
The old and new confusions made *them* less.

Their talent and their passion too unfocused,
Too split between tradition and progression,
They could not think or feel quite right, so missed
The chance to make the abstract concrete, their obsession:
To parrot what they'd heard—so dour.
But Dad just laughed, "That wasn't worth an hour!"

My Uncle made an ódd statement before
We loaded up the van to drive back home.

"We never would have traveled out this far—
Unless we were the kind of men to roam—
To play and sing for nothing, like we do,
Before the day the Interstate came through.

"And yet, new things like this, connecting worlds,
Will likely mean the death of what we love:
This Bluegrass. Because Folk belongs to worlds
Of people who must lean on what they have.
Now, we don't need it; we just love it, so
Bluegrass will fade away like all things do."

I don't play music like I did
Before I left to move across the country.
My dusty Gibson F-5 sits beneath its lid
Unless I use it to spark creativity.
I sold my Martin HD-28 guitar
While saving for a house and car.

But the poet Bashō wrote it well:
The seed of music and of thought took root
Decades ago; the vines bear flowers still. That smell
Brings back old times—the clear notes of a flute.
Or in my case, the notes of fiddles, banjos,
Guitars, mandolins, and upright basses.

Now, Tony Rice and Ricky Skaggs do it,
Transporting me back to the Ozark hills,
Or when my brother Seth and I duet—
Guitars come out, we flex old skills.
Our Dad and Uncle Malcolm were our masters,
Both helping us avoid the old and new disasters.

We drove back home at midnight, a three-hour drive,
But had no trouble being on the lookout.
We nearly had a wreck, were glad to be alive—
An eighteen-wheeler had a blowout,
But Dad drove for a living, swerved just right,
And brought us safely home that night.

www.ingramcontent.com/pod-product-compliance
Lightning Source LLC
Chambersburg PA
CBHW061455040426
42450CB00007B/1372

"Ethan McGuire's *Apocalypse Dance* is a collection of poetry that uses all of history as its subject and all of humanity as its theme. We feel the cold and the warmth of his textured images and recognize the sentiment behind each word, whether he speaks of ancient times or of his American hometown. McGuire's love of music seeps into his poems and gives them depth and dimension. His words read like lyrics—rich with detail, raw with emotion, and ripe with meaning."

—**JEANNIE ZOKAN**, author of *The Existence of Pity*

"*Apocalypse Dance* is indeed always dancing. It dances with Christianity, Taoism, and Buddhism. It dances through spiritual geography, through relationship issues (with God and others), through reworkings of song lyrics and translations from Classical Chinese. It is always thrumming with the passionate fascination McGuire brings to all he captures."

—**AARON POOCHIGIAN**, author of *Mr. Either/Or*

"Ethan McGuire's debut work of poetry, *Apocalypse Dance*, is a beautiful collection of short poems that sings to the heart and soul of the human condition. A splendid book which features how poems of all sizes can be beautiful, the reader is entreated to couplets, tercets, quatrains, and sonnets that make the reader want to sing and dance with what they are reading. The gentle reader might just be welcomed into eternity with the poems that Ethan McGuire has decided to share with the world."

—**PAUL KRAUSE**, editor of *VoegelinView*

"These are honest, heartfelt poems. Inspired by ancient writers, modern-day musicians, friendship, love, and the sheer strangeness of daily life, they ask clear-eyed questions about 'what has been, what is, will be.' McGuire avoids easy solace in his answers, instead working toward conclusions that are less certain and more true. He's also willing to be playful, keeping us on the hook with variations in mood and form. Whether deftly translating a Song dynasty sage, attentively cataloguing a hurricane's aftermath, or quietly noting his exact distance from home, this is a poet who is always writing for one simple reason: his love of poetry."

—**ALICE ALLAN**, host of *Poetry Says*

"Ethan McGuire's poetry and writings have been thought provoking and a joy to read over the years. He began contributing to Fevers of the Mind six years ago. I have seen him grow in his comfort with imagery to become one of the most intelligent wordsmiths in the game. Ethan's influences are shown through the many wonderful lyricists that influence so many: Leonard Cohen, C. S. Lewis, Sylvia Plath, Bob Dylan, Neil Young, Joni Mitchell, other prophets of word. Ethan's vast knowledge of history and the issues of the current day put you in the moment."

—**DAVID L. O'NAN**, publisher, Fevers of the Mind website

"Ethan McGuire takes us from the neon lights and pulsing music of clubs to the silence of starry skies. He takes us from his ancestral Ozarks to Bashō's Japan (bringing both together in his remarkable long poem "The Bluegrass Players"). This is an impressive full-collection debut from a versatile poet and translator with a musician's ear."

—**STEVEN KNEPPER**, editor, *New Verse Review: A Journal of Lyric and Narrative Poetry*